I0004925

Freq'ed Out

Extravagant Publications, LLC is registered in the United States Patent and Trademark Office.

All **Extravagant Publications, LLC.** Titles, Imprints and Distributed Lines are available at special quantity discounts for bulk purchases for sales promotions, premiums, fundraising and educational or institutional use.

Imprint: *Extravagant Publications, LLC.*

www.Extravagant Publications, LLC.com

ISBN: 9781087878850

Acknowledgments:

I like to thank all of my families for being there for me. All the friends, who have waited so long for the book to be in print. I like to thank all of the 1st responders in the ongoing fight of the coronavirus pandemic of 2020. And a especial thanks to the Baptist Memorial Hospital staff for helping me during and after my heart surgery on Mar 9th. The Dr and Nursing staff of this hospital , I will always be grateful too. Thanks to Johnson Controls team for allowing me into their working family.

Without Earth's foundation none of this is possible, so now I will use what I have learned as a gift to educate others.

Lamonte Jordan – Graphics

GruvyGraffics.com

Ronnie D. Johnson Bio

Nickname: Ronnnamm

At the age of fifty-one, Ronnie D. Johnson has had a many titles added to his name - not all of them good, but the experiences outweigh the persona. He started his career out as a teenager in the US Navy aboard the super carrier John F. Kennedy. After a four year career onboard the ship, he ended his enlistment and return to his home in Memphis, Tn. He started to pursue a career in music while working for ADT Security Company. While working for ADT , Ronnie found a passion for computers and started to develop his skills using technology as his focal point.

After leaving ADT, Ronnie acquired a position with the City of Memphis Police Department. Ronnie used his amazing skills of technology and his uncanny knack to finish what he started to propel himself to the upper level of the department that he was assigned to. After leaving the police dept.

Ronnie put together a fictional persona that he made up loosely based on himself. "Frequency Hunter" would be Ronnie's alternate ego with an unlimited potential of growth and depth. Frequency Hunter is a mix between Microsoft (Bill Gates), who he greatly respects with a touch of MacGyver and a Navy Seal. As Ronnie life progressed his quest to bring "Frequency Hunter" to print began. After starting a successful business, working a fulltime job, plus dealing with the day to day antics of his two gorgeous children (Eboni and Ronnie Jr). Ronnie D. Johnson has brought to print a multitude of stories that will entice your passion to read.

Freq'ed Out

By

Ronnie D. Johnson

Table of Contents

1. Pantha Pack

2. Posed

3. Hostile Coup

4. Bookworm

5. ASSassIn

6. Awakened into a Bad Dream

7. Broken the #1 Rule

8. Never Dead, Always Upgraded

9. On Board CyberEye

10. K. O. KnockOut

11. Volcano

Pantha Pack

Eyes had been sending the pack communication equipment to his cousin EoW for some serious adjustments. EoW told Eyes that he couldn't make the changes to government equipment, but he could send him the diy of how to upgrade the equipment to something more viable for the job. Eyes thanked his cousin and moved on to get his crew ready for the last run of a series, and some welcome rest.

The President needed this particular crew to not do well on this last mission. This was one of the crews mentioned in one of the briefing that could mess up his plans and rally the troops around, whoever they chose. The President had some serious hard intel that the leader of the crew was going to make a run for the Presidency, and he had no plans of ever leaving his post. Mr. President had put together a very elaborate plan to put him and his family into American power for as long as he had a heir in this world. Mr. President had decided that the election process was a waste of time and it was time for him, to show everyone, who is BOSS.

The expedite crew had their orders and were assemble post haste and dropped into the hostile zone. Kahuna gave his 5-man crew rolling orders and explicit rules that came from top down. Kahuna cleared his mind of all his future plans and concentrated on everyone getting home safe. Kahuna had the guys double check all the gear and was immediately told by Eyes that the new combat communication gear from Space Force Industries was glitchy. Bhang was having a problem with the fitment of his vocal piece, Grounds equipment had cracks throughout the system and Fly was just some static filled headphones.

Kahuna rallied his crew and promised them, when they made it through this last one, they would no longer have to ever worry about SFI products again.

The plane signaled the crew and they were dropped into the hot zone. Fly immediately went to find the aircraft they could use for extraction. Grounds went out and started setting up for whatever they needed to have a clean getaway. Eyes made his way to higher ground release the surveillance drones so that the crew could have vision on all the situations.

Bhang went deep into the motor pool to secure a vehicle for extraction. Kahuna had full details of the area they were in and he came up with the best extraction point.

Eyes made it to the setup place, and everything was incorrect. Something else was already working and it was not looking good. Eyes immediately tried to signal the guys but the SFI equipment just would not connect. Eyes pulled his mini Glock setup and immediately released the drones. He quickly assembles the assault setup and prepared himself for a serious defense. The drones were preprogrammed and headed for the proper positioning, they were immediately targeted and were shot down. Eyes had always setup his drones in secret so that the powers that be wouldn't know about this alert mechanism. The crew immediately tried to communicate but the SFI equipment fell apart as they tried to use it. Kahuna immediately went into rally of the crew phase. He and the guys always trained on this scenario just in case they were caught in an EMP blast. Each man knew what to do so Kahuna was confident that they would be ok. Each man heard the drones explode which let them know that the mission had been aborted.

Grounds snatched off all the SFI gear and tossed it into a 50-gallon drum. He locked and loaded his weapon and immediately started to set himself for an advantage point. They all used specialized weapons, but they would not be enough to hold off a small army for long. Grounds used some of the old school natural camouflage to conceal his whereabouts. He did not make a sound but maintained a visual to help arrived.

Bhang had just made it to the motor pool when he heard the explosions. He quickly tried to communicate but SFI gear fell apart.

Bhang had suspicion that they had been setup and now they needed to battle to survive. Bhang immediately got all his weapons ready and found something that was very odd. A military Striker was there totally riddled with bullets. He moved around and found more and more in the same shape. The under belly was riddled with bullets but none of them penetrated the armor. Bhang became agitated and scared at the same time. Someone was using 250k guns on small armies.

Bhang was about to move to go rally the crew when all hell broke loose and he had to handle these goons as only he could, body bag cold.

Fly was up to his neck in bullshit trying to fend off the goons defending the flight line. After the explosion they came out of now where and he had to handle business until something better came along. Fly slipped and fell into what must've been an underground hanger. He gained his focus and saw what had to be a figment of his imagination. It was an old A7 Corsair that was fully fueled and armed. Fly didn't have time for formalities and he quickly had the plane ready to be airborne. All his flight checks were a go so he pressed the garage door opener and awaited the results.

 The merc were not prepared for what they saw as the doors opened there was a jet plane running. Fly saw that the plane could move out of the hangar and he proceeded to get the bird in the air. He was met with some small arms fire but one quick push on the throttle blew them clear. Fly unfolded the wings of the A7 immediately got it in the air. Quick inventory of the armament let Fly know he could do enough to get the guys out of there, but nothing over the top. He had to be conservative but deadly.

Kahuna was pissed they had been declared collateral damage. He knew exactly who was responsible for this and he was going to make them pay. Kahuna had a lot on the line, and he knew what was at stake. He moved throughout the grid and he was taken out mercs as he made his way to the extraction point. Kahuna was taken back as he was hit with an audible device. He quickly ran behind a building and shed all his SFI equipment. Everything was falling apart and SFI was a key factor into what was happening. Kahuna checked all of his gear and he found just what was needed. He quickly assembled the combat bow and decided to do a little eradicating. His 1st shot hit the audible guy in his right cheek bone pinning him to the truck bed. The next shot took out the driver. Kahuna moved quickly and took the truck to look for his crew. Kahuna knew Eyes was the one guy on his crew that didn't have all the necessary training for survival. Kahuna immediately headed for him. Grounds and Bhang had the same fore thoughts and they headed in the same vicinity. All three men fought and battled to the area where Eyes was supposed to be. They somehow made it at the same time to see a horrible sight. Eyes had been tortured to death. His hands were pulled tight behind him and his legs were spread. Someone had stabbed him several times with electrode until he died. Then to make matters worth they burned out both of his eyes.

The crew lost it, they collected his body and then began the tremendous task of getting back home. Bhang grabbed his weapons and took lead, while Kahuna carried the body of their fallen comrade. Grounds secured the rear as they moved with haste to the airfield. Bhang motioned to the crew to get under the Striker vehicles. The piercing sound was the alert that someone was about to fire the 250k gun. As they barely made it behind the vehicle the guns fired. Four 250k guns fired 1 million rounds decimating everything under that canvas.

Fly targeted all four guns and lay waste to them. Kahuna was the 1st to break cover. Everything was shredded from those guns. Kahuna hurried found an old cart and he put the body of Eyes onto it. He quickly found Bhang and Grounds; they both had been hit superficially but would survive. Kahuna was injured and didn't have time to assess his on damages, but he knew he had to get them out of there. He loaded the cart with the rest of the crew, and he made way to the flight area, where he knew they could find their way home.

Fly landed the A7 and taxied it just short of a private helicopter. He was surprised this thing was here until he met up with Kahuna. Kahuna filled him in on all the bullshit and the two of them decided to leave in a pop goes the weasel exit strategy. As they secured everybody into the helicopter, Fly and Kahuna was met with small arm fire. Fly was shot in the back of the leg and he collapsed into the helicopter. Kahuna hurriedly got the helicopter in the air and Grounds pushed the button as he sang pop goes the weasel. All their set munitions exploded in a perfect symphony which cleared the way for Kahuna to fly them out of harms way. Kahuna looked back at them knowing that his new fight would be to find out, who set them up for collateral damage.

Metal Storm 250k

Posed

    1 year has passed since the pack has made it back home. They all decided to go their separate ways to heal and then regroup. Bhang got stitched up and immediately wanted to get himself back into the gym. He was an advent physical specimen and his fighting skills were 2nd to none. Bhang went into his local gym in Michigan and they had the news on talking about how the President was making some serious threats to Muslim nation to cease fire and take care of their people. Bhang walked away from the tv and started his

warmup exercises. Victoria Justice had booked the entire spa for herself and her staff to have a spa day. She walked in and noticed a man that was not on her staff roster. Victoria immediately went to the spa owner and reminder her that she had paid for an exclusive day and someone was violating their agreement. The spa owner told Victoria to follow her and they would get to the bottom of it. As soon as the spa owner saw that it was Bhang she turned to Victoria and offered her a full refund. Victoria was stubborn and told the owner that she wanted her day as they planned, and she was not changing because of some over the top gym rat. Bhang heard the ladies talking and decided he would interject his thoughts into the situation. Bhang walked up to the owner and asked her to step aside and allow him to fix the problem. Victoria immediately began a to get this man out of the gym. Bhang walked up to Victoria and introduced himself. Victoria decided that she wanted to meet him in another atmosphere later but would tolerate him for now. Bhang tried to accommodate Alexandria concerns and they kept bumping into one another as they tried to use this private gym facility. Victoria decided it was time for Bhang and his serious gym exercises. Victoria went and got a bucket of Ice and Icey Hot muscle rub. Bhang had just finished on one of the machines Victoria was using, but he didn't put it back on the settings she had. Victoria had enough and she told Bhang she was about to teach Bhang a lesson. Bhang laughed out loud because he thought that was hilarious. He turned his back on Victoria and she struck quickly before Bhang could stop her. Victoria grabbed a handful of the Icey hot rub and jammed her hands down into Bhang's shorts rubbing the Icey Hot across his genitals. Bhang grabbed her hand, but it was too late. The icy hot brung him to his knees. Victoria straddled Bhang and made him agree to dinner with her. Bhang was in pain and had to agree to her demands. Victoria helped him up and told him not to be late. Bhang was on fire and he was not going to let her get away with this. Just as he thought she was done; she pulled the back of his workout shorts and dumped ice in it. Bhang let out a high-pitched scream as he dropped to his knees. Victoria was all fun and games, now because she had secured a date for night. She bent down and whispered into Bhang ear, that he should wear something nice and he better not be late. Bhang got up off the floor and rushed to the shower to hurriedly get this massage rub off his jewels. As he thought about his latest situation, he basically got outsmarted by the Victoria woman and now she literally had him by the balls.

Fly couldn't believe how bad of shape he was in. His lady had him babysitting their pet because he went and bought a plane with his own money. Feathers let out one of his calls to let Fly know he wanted a snack. Feathers had grown to double the size of any bird that Fly had ever seen. The big sea eagle was found by Fly when he was a newbie. Someone had cut down the tree that had his nest in it. Fly decided to keep the little bird and now he had one of the biggest birds known to man as a pet. Fly loved taking Feathers to aeronautical shows as a conversation piece, but his main reason was keeping in the know of all the latest aeronautical innovations and sometimes they would take him for ride. Lady Fly didn't care if Fly would ever fly again. She was just happy he was home safe. The last time he came home bleeding and all she could do was patch him up and get him back on his feet. Lady Fly walked in on Fly picking with his last set of wounds. She picked up a fly swatter and hit on the hand. Fly grabbed his lady and started kissing her, but was interrupted by Feathers flapping his wings and calling for a treat. Fly and his lady took care of the bird and got themselves some food as they discussed the airplane Fly decided to purchase. Fly explained to his lady that he wanted to be able to do some island hopping and to take

Feathers to the veterinarian to see about getting that bad wing fixed. Lady Fly knew he was using it for an excuse, but they did need to get Feathers wing fixed. Lady Fly agreed to let him keep it, if he got it retrofitted for Feathers to ride on the outside . Fly remembered that salesman and immediately gave him a call. The price for a bird that size was expensive. And the only way Fly was going to be able to fly his new plane, is get this setup paid for. Fly gave told Lady Fly he was going out for a ride. He kissed her and got into his car, then headed out to see an old friend.

Kahuna was working out as usual, he and his pet seal Slick decided they would hang out in the gym today. Kahuna had a small blowup swimming pool that he rolled around with him to keep Slick cool. Kahuna took Slick everywhere with him. Slick kept him grounded and levelheaded. Lady Kahuna enjoyed having them two together all the time. Slick kept Kahuna out of trouble and Kahuna loved that seal for it. Lady Kahuna finished fixing lunch for her crew, saw she rang the gong to let them know it was time to eat. Kahuna told Slick to get in his ride, because it is time to eat and they both didn't want to get in trouble.

Slick wobbled into the pool and Kahuna pulled him to the house so that they could get them some nourishment.

Kahuna had this thought on his mind for some time, and now was the moment for him to enter the realm of politics. He wouldn't hold back his tenacity to be the best, so he decided to push this political dream all the way to the top. Now he had to convince his wife and crew that this was a good thing.

Hostile Coup

The crowd was at awe at the voter turnout. The USA would have a new president. The poles and the news media were elated. The mayor of Hawaii had done the inevitable, he had become the new president of the USA . The Kahuna / Justice ticket was an unstoppable force that the preceding President didn't see coming.

Kahuna and his committee were celebrating and enjoying the results. He ran as an independent and he was able to convince the USA that he could fix the problems which was the current President and his family.

Thumpf and his family was nowhere to be found. They had begun a serious takeover of the American government. 1st thing Thumpf did was make sure at all the gatherings the Metal Storm Firing mechanism disguised as lighting systems. Each array was filled with thousands of pathogen virus capsules. Thumpf figured the people can't put him out of office, if they were too busy dying of this virus. 2nd he contacted Abu MaHoodi the brother of Jahoodi and gave him exclusive movement in and out of the USA. Thumpf had SOD and SOA in his pocket because they had nasty gambling and whoring debts that he bought out. Next, he had his daughter Irmina to handle the Thumpf family businesses and ensure all of the communist leaders had substantial debts to ensure that they would be at his beck and call, when he decided not to surrender the Presidentcy. Dolphus and Errol Thumpf had swindled their way onto the hierarchy of CEO boards for SFI (Space Force Indus.) and its conglomerates. The boys had reduced the equipment to basically over paid tracking devices that was basically, a targeting system for the

Metal Storm Firing array. The boys then used their status to setup Metal storm all over the world at every major event arena.

They knew they had a big chance of losing the Presidentcy, but that didn't mean that their dad had to stop being President.

Bhang hugged his woman in a congratulatory way. She and Kahuna were now President and Vice President Elect. Victoria thought about what just happened and she cried in the arms of the man that was there for her all the way. The two of them broke their embraced kissed and went to stand next the entity that had taken the world by storm. D.J. Kahuna was an emotional wreck he was on his knees giving a prayer in Samoan then he stood and put some clothes on to go and allow everyone to celebrate with him and his staff.

The announcer made the announcement and the winning presidentcy ticket Kahuna and Justice stepped out on stage to a roaring crowd of millions. As soon as Kahuna went to speak at the podium, the coup fired the Metal Storm Array filled with the virus. People scattered and started screaming, the virus worked fast as the mist flew the crowd. All the screens throughout the viewing public showed the President with a smirk on his face. Thumpf immediately sent in the military and had the world put on lockdown. Everyone knew it was some kind of terrorist weapon and now the new president and staff was affected by the results.

Soon as the cameras shutoff the Thumpf contacted his two older sons and let them pass the message to the business partners , that the USA would continue business as usual. Thumpf then had secret service make sure that his family would escort to his private club to ensure that they would be in an environment he could control.

Labrador Ratcliffe bka LabRat had expanded his repertoire that he was now among apart of young elitist that had become a part of the Secret Service. LabRat had endured all the physical training like it was a walk in the park.

He decided to spend more time with old Thunderhead, and it paid off.

Thunderhead had LabRat training like he was going to be a Seal team special op. LabRat excelled in all the obstacle training that the CIA and FBI threw at him. LabRat even used a few tricks from the shadow team to show off some computer skills to make the instructor go back and ask questions. LabRat excelled and graduated top of his class. He now was assigned to the White House and everything was in turmoil. LabRat was assigned as a part of the Presidential escort of the President two youngest children, Telsa and Bernhard. These two were night and day in comparison, but equally their fathers children. Telsa was estranged from her father until he won the Presidentcy and Bernhard was the baby boy that was spoiled and justified heir of his father's billions.

LabRat knew he could not use any unauthorized tech within these walls because it would be considered a crime against the oath he had taken as a Secret Service agent. Still LabRat had problems with all the underhanded tactics that were happening around him.

LabRat went into the White House on his usual scheduled duty, but was immediately reassigned to carry some very important information . The briefcase was handcuffed to his risk and he was told by his commander stay within the RedZone unless otherwise notified. LabRat was immediately escorted into the Oval office where the President was finishing up some important business. The briefcase was unhandcuffed from LabRat and he was told to have a seat in a particular room until notified. LabRat exited the door directly into the Blue Zone, where a different Secret Service commander sat him down and explained everything to him. Since the new President elect was out of commission they were put on hold as his official escort until all this calamity is figured out.

He was told that Thumpf was inciting a coup and issuing martial law to issue in his new Dictatorship. Thumpf was a main suspect in the unleashing of the virus pandemic that was sweeping the Nation, but there was no proof of his or his crew involvement.

LabRat thought about all the conspiracy stories Thunderhead had told him about, so he knew that he had to figure out something that could make things right.

LabRat knew there was someone who could make this right, but no one had heard from him in over five years. LabRat then started to ask the Secret Service commander, what was he supposed to do until the new President is in place where he belongs.

The commander stated that the acknowledge briefcase was in Thumpf's care and without that, the new President would not have access to anything , except a press conference. The commander told LabRat that everything was preset before the attack and once that briefcase crosses the threshold from the red zone. Then the new President is technically in power. LabRat now understood why that brief was so damn important. Not just any old briefcase but the acknowledgement of a new political power in the White House.

Bookworm

LabRat was now very involved into a plan to get things back right in the White House. He had been in the room with Bernhard Thumpf and the kid was throwing a temper tantrum because he didn't want to go out to his father golf club. He hated it there and he could move around like in the White House. As a Secret Service agent assigned to him LabRat learned that the President was involved with shaking down a group of female Senators that were talking against him. Thumpf had his sons put out a 500k bounty on anyone, who had dirt about these female senators. LabRat could not go to any ethics committee, because Thumpf already had most of everybody in his pocket. There was no way he could pass this information without having his new career hung out to dry. LabRat then remembered how he would get dirt on everyone in school, by just being a bookworm that had people running their mouths as he helped them make it through school.

LabRat had to reach deep and find patience in the process. He was sure if Frequency was able, he would have no problem with helping him. But that whole network had been shut down and all the people had scattered after Thumpf got in office.

LabRat really started to wonder if Thumpf had anything to do with Frequency disappearance. Another notion LabRat would work on once he figured out, how to get the current situation ratified.

Bernhard screamed at the 1st Lady that his dad and all his cronies could go hump a camel in the desert. His mother laughed then slapped Bernhard across the cheek knocking him to the floor. Mrs. Thumpf then scolded Bernhard that who his father meets in his private meetings, should stay private. Bernhard was shocked but acknowledged his mother in agreement. After Mrs. Thumpf left, Bernhard decided to get a little revenge against his mother for hitting him. LabRat was obligated to follow Bernhard everywhere he went and had a hard in place rule not to touch them unless it was absolutely necessary. LabRat saw his opportunity, so he decided to add a simple worm mentor program to Bernhard cell. This program would answer all of the voice command questions and also help Bernhard make decisions, whenever he requested it. It would be an easy way to use one of Thumpf's kids to help him find out what was really going on.

Bernhard decided to take a nap before he went out on his

mischievous run. He emptied his pockets and laid his cell on the nightstand next to his bed. LabRat waited for about an hour then he made his move. He slipped into the kid's bedroom and loaded the program on his phone so effortlessly. LabRat then slipped back out to his post, like he had never left. The commander of the secret service walked into the hall and found LabRat cleaning something off his shoes. He approached LabRat and asked him was everything alright. LabRat pulled the chewing gum from his shoe and told the commander that he fell victim to one of Bernhard pranks. The commander laughed and called for another agent to replace

LabRat until he got himself cleaned up. The commander told LabRat to take the rest of the day off and send him the bill for the chewing gum cleaning. LabRat acknowledged and immediately clocked out and went home. Thanks to Bernhard and his pranks, he could now get started on a plan to get answers to the chaotic situation, they were currently in.

Bernhard awoke from his nap, took a shower , then went to get some food and revenge. As he made it to the kitchen, he was met by one of his father's agents and was instructed that Thumpf wanted to see him immediately. Bernhard went to his dad and gave him a hug.

Thumpf told Bernhard that he was not to have any more chewing gum in the agent's quarters. Bernhard said ok, then his dad told him that he heard about his mother slapping him. Bernhard knew that he was in trouble, so he sat down on the couch and waited for his dad to add injury to insult. Thumpf told Bernhard to hand him that silver briefcase that was sitting on the floor. Bernhard did as requested, and his dad started rambling on, about how the other characters trying to take over from him, didn't listen to him when he said , there would be dire consequences to anyone that didn't listen to him. He slammed the briefcase on the desk as a way to ensure his son Bernhard was paying attention to him. Thumpf then had Bernhard come over to him and gave him a big hug. He whispered into Bernhard ear don't make me ever have to raise my voice at you again, understand. A very frightened Bernhard acknowledged his father and then an Agent came in with some burgers and fries. The father and son sat in silence as they enjoyed their meal. Bernhard thought of getting even with his mom was totally gone and now he would get himself ready to head out to the golf club.

Thumpf was having a moment, this one was about a few women political leaders going against his commands. Thumpf for some odd reason like grabbing the silver briefcase and using it for his personal frustration devices. After beating the briefcase on the floor, he threw against the wall, for good measure. By that time the Secretary of State walked in and the two of them had a private meeting, of what to do to make this issue from the ladies go bye bye. Thumpf was assured by the Secretary, that this crew could get the job done and make a spectacle out of the situation. The embarrassment alone, will put a muzzle on these women and set at ease some of their rivals. Thumpf gave the Secretary the green light on the plan, and had funding sent through various channels to keep the White House totally out of being implicated once the deeds have been performed.

ASSassIn

The street business had been booming, since the disappearance of Frequency Hunter and his crew. Most of the street business went unopposed thanks to the way the politicians handled the special enforcement teams. Ms. Bobbi was bouncing around her chateau awaiting some news from the last money drop, her girls was taking care of. The three women showed up and gave Ms. Bobbi nothing but good news. They started to celebrate the fortunate news that told them, the church that bought their old club was being shutdown and the good Pastor was being held for murder. As the story was told, the Pastor found out that his new wife had been sleeping around with a lot of the men and women of the congregation. She was blackmailing them to help fund some of her very expensive trips out of the country. She also was buying a lot of pure bronze, silver, and gold bars with the illegal money. The Pastor found out through one of the LGBTQ committee chairs. The Pastor had all the culprits meet him at the church for a special meeting and poisoned them all. He had his wife, show up a little later and he called out to her "Madame", then he shot her point blank in the face.

Ms. Bobbi laughed because she could not stand Madame in any form or fashion. She always wanted to kill her, but the street code always saved her. Now it was time to take over the Pastor business when a group of men came in to deliver a message. Ms. Bobbi knew these guys was well trained and covert. She dared not make a move. Ms. Bobbi took the message and just as fast as they came in, they were gone.

Ms. Bobbi assigned the hit to her "triple threat assassins". Gold , Silver and Bronze were a deadly trio that left murder and mayhem in their wake. Not once had they let her down and this particular hit needed to be precise.

Each target was setup according to their secret little habit. The first lady had a pension for little girls, so they let Silver trick her into spending money to sleep with her daughter. To the ladies surprise, Silver and her co-harts ,they exposed the senator to Silver's extra gifts and made sure they had plenty of video to cover the plan. Silver finished the Senator off and then hung the body like an animal carcass. This will be a message sent to ensure not to try and double cross them. The second lady had a BDSM habit. She loved finding young boys and exploiting

Their needs to allow her to beat them into submission. Gold used her talents to set the lady up and the three of them beat her with a 9tails whips and exposed her via video to the public eye, hung out to dry.

The 3rd and last one was going to be very difficult, but Bronze had the ideal just to break into her home and let her try to run. They did just that and the lady's 300+ pound figure was to much for her. She felled over and over again as she became short of breath. Bronze found a pair of scissors and started cutting the clothes off this lady until she was totally naked. The lady screamed at them, who she was and that she was a very powerful woman. Bronze laughed at her as she poured corn oil all over her. The lady laughed and stated to them, that they could not use this as blackmail, because she was an openly gay professional and this is just a little nonsense. Bronze, Gold and Silver exposed themselves to her as transgendered and made her understand that she would not be walking away from this night. She was the only victim not found hung up, but her body was beaten and abused till the end.

As the 3 assassins showed back up to the hotel. Ms. Bobbi was there to meet them. She immediately had them clean up and go into hiding until she gave the coast clear. Ms. Bobbi then sent a message to her connect that he needs to make payments, because the little nuisance had been taken care of permanently.

The Secretary of State was sent an undisclosed package. He opened it up and the only thing in it was a microSD card. He used his secret service approve adapter to insert the card into his computer. He clicked on one of the videos and saw one of the nuisances being whipped and brutalized by a gold skinned woman, or that was until she started to rape and sodomize her victim. The Secretary of State knew what to expect from the other two videos, so he went to find President Thumpf. Thumpf was throwing another temper tantrum at a press conference, because one of the reporters was questioning about his legitimacy. Thumpf got so furious he had all the press escorted out of the media room. Thumpf then finished giving the statements that he wanted to give and then walked out of the media room blowing a kiss to a bunch of empty green chairs. As soon as he was out of the room, he immediately had the video engineers add a cheering audience to his press conference. The Secretary of State walked up to Thumpf and let him know that his nuisances had been taken care of. Thumpf nodded and told him to close out our agreement as we discussed.

The Secretary of State sent the finish order and the secret service hit squad closed the deal.

All of Ms. Bobbi's enemies and competitors were taken out with extreme prejudice. Roz and Mynt were blown up in their own warehouse. The GayMack was shot up with heroin until his eyes dam near popped out of his head. All the street gangs were mowed down in a hail of Metal Storm firepower. No one was left alive to compete or give Ms. Bobbi a problem with running the streets.

Ms. Bobbi laughed as she got a big courier box delivered to her chateau. She opened it up and it contained the recipe for the Lickem drugs, all of the gang's client info, and 3 million dollars in cash for taken care of those three nuisances.

Ms. Bobbi let out a big laugh and told all the people inside to turn the music up and let's party. There has been a new Queen of the city anointed and now let's set this turn this muthafucka upside down.

Awakened into a Bad Dream

Kahuna could barely move; he
tried to talk and move his arm but he
was secured to the bed. He like the
rest of the crew were all in the same
predicament. Immediately, Fly called
out for his wife, but she was not
there. Grounds was busy trying to
escape from his bed, when he heard
a whistle from Bhang. All the men
stopped struggling and paid attention
to the TV. Since they had been
knocked out and exposed to the
virus, Thumpf had been running the
country like a dictator and anyone

that tried to confront him, was handled with extreme prejudice.

The whole crew was trying to come up with a way to escape, when they heard the guards dropped to the floor. The door opened and old Thunderhead walked into the room. He held a very strong stun device in his hands and told the crew, that they must be quiet. He then went to each man and ran a scanner over their body until it squealed. He then covered the area with HVAC tape. Once he did that to each man, he then freed them from their beds. Thunderhead then explained to them that they had been shot with listening and tracking devices. He told them that they could now move and speak freely until they could get the devices safely removed. Grounds was pissed and he wanted to know, who did this to them. Kahuna had a feeling, but he would not speculate until he had the facts. Bhang decided to keep quiet until he could put his hands on the culprit. Fly was ready to go but he was still a little lightheaded from the virus. Thunderhead handed Kahuna a map and a radio. He told them to follow the instructions and do not deviate. Kahuna asked Thunderhead, who was it that was helping them and Thunderhead proudly told them, that it was his Godson and he is working from inside of the Whitehouse.

Kahuna promised Thunderhead that when all this is over, he would make sure he and his godson would be greatly taken care of. Thunderhead told the guys to get a move on before they notice the guards have been taken out and you all are on the run. Bhang grabbed the paper from Kahuna and headed out of the building as was described on the paper. Grounds brung up the rear making sure he left small little booby traps to buy them more time on their escape. The plan went without a hitch and the crew headed to the pickup point for further directions.

As they walked into the small building, they were met with small compartments with their names on it. Each place was like a small apartment with all the amenities. Each man had a Kriss Vector combat system fitted to them and their style of combat. All the men sat down and learned the combat system after they showered and shaved. Once they finished training and familiarizing themselves with the system, they came into the common area to work on a plan to rescue everyone from this political coup. Fly was really in a zone and he had to tell the crew, what he was feeling. Kahuna asked Fly what was wrong, and Fly told them that they were flying somewhere?

Kahuna was confused until they got a communication message. It said the team would be dropped into an undisclosed area. Once the doors are open, the crew should not ask any questions but drop any persons not affiliated with the team. Failure is not an option and this mission will be a tide turner to bringing an end to this mess. Kahuna addressed his crew and told them to get ready to put this combat system to test.

The crew went to their cabins and got fully dressed in the combat system. As soon as the container touched ground the system came online. The crew was amazed at the technology that appeared in front of their eyes. Each system had data fed directly to an eyepiece. They saw the men walking up the door and open them up with a boom. As the dust cleared from the explosion one of the doors was wedged in between the building blast doors keeping them from closing. The crew hurriedly made their way into the building and down the corridors. The crew was dropping bodies as they made their way to the center of the building, where there was some kind of high-tech prison.

Kahuna had heard about these things and thought that it was all science fiction mumbo jumbo. They made it to the main holding area where Bhang was given instructions to knock out the guard but do not kill him. Bhang went into the room and was met with a big Turk, who was not happy with the visit. The two men went at it and Bhang took a slight beating but was victorious.

Grounds walked over to Bhang and tapped on his watch. Bhang asked Grounds what was wrong, Grounds laughed and said, you rusty he lasted too long. They all had a good laugh and then the next message came over the screen. They were instructed to put the Turk hand and face up the screen to activate the system. They were then told to search for a certain prisoner that had on a radioactive protective suit. The system came online, and the pods started moving around very quickly.

The pod stopped and the system asked the question was it ok to release the pod. Kahuna hit yes and the pod was placed on the release deck. The system announced that all non-essential personnel should take cover behind protected areas and then it released the contents of the pod. A human shaped body slid from out of the pod, it was green and slightly glowing. Grounds got a message to take the jumper cables and batteries the guards have been using for torture and hook them onto this body anywhere. Grounds did as was instructed and then he turned the juice on. The body shook hard and then let out this weird scream. The batteries drained quickly and then the body stood up. The green glow went away and then they heard a voice that was not expected. The voice told the crew that an extraction team would be there any second and they should ready themselves for extraction.

Fly went to Kahuna and asked him, what the green hell is going on. Kahuna had no ideal, but he was not going to let this glow rod just come and take over. As soon as they were about to confront the green thing, Grounds yelled out they had company. The crew started taking on the assault, but they lost the green thing in the melee. Before they could ask what happen to him, they heard the blast of heavy munitions and a minigun. The green thing had contacted his source and they sent in the Devil Dawgs. These fully automated robotic combat systems were doing exactly what they were designed for. The crew saw these robotic dogs destroy anything that came at them and then they followed the green thing to this flying ship called the Airfish. The Airfish was being flown by another robot that was call CamShaft. The crew was instructed to buckle in and hold on tight. The Airfish took off vertically and was flying across the sea effortlessly. Fly was amazed at this flight technology. He leaned over to Kahuna and said I don't know who these people are, but they have got to get me one of these. Kahuna laughed but he was also nervous, because he was sitting behind a green thing that was radioactive.

CamShaft announced to the crew that they were docking on the ship and the crew would be shown to their quarters for debriefing. They followed the robot to each of their uniquely design quarters. As each of the men finished showering, they were told to get into the rough sea seats because they were about to run into a storm. Each man did as instructed and climbed into the seats and fell asleep.

The green thing as he was called started the Inoculation program. The program basically stripped him of all the radioactive power and nanosource. The power was directed into the reactor of the ship and then it was restarted for a whole new look and plenty of upgrades. The new ship was now called CyberEye and DocBot was a true AI hospital hologram program. DocBot immediately, came online and got all of the men bandage up and tracing devices removed. DocBot then cleaned all the green stuff off of Frequency Hunter.

Kahuna, Fly, Bhang and Grounds awoke to some body aches. They were immediately dressed and escorted to the main eating area to meet the person behind this. They were shocked when Frequency walked into the room and greeted them. The crew was confused but were satisfied that a human was behind all this. Frequency then explained how he ended up as the green thing that they rescued. He then explained how he was double crossed by the Thumpf family. Kahuna hit the table and stated that some bitch going to pay. Frequency then had DocBot give them the devices that had been placed inside of them as tracing devices. Each man started checking their bodies and making sure nothing else was going on. Bhang was hot, he wanted to get even, and his patience was wearing thin. Frequency asked the men how many people that they knew personally that Thumpf had control over. Kahuna stated he has our wives. Frequency then asked Kahuna could he join them to help take out Thumpf and clean up this chaos.

Grounds pulled Kahuna to the side and asked him, how do we know that we can trust this guy. By the time, Kahuna was about to answer Eyeball decided he wanted to see his old friend. CamShaft called over the intercom system Eyeball on port side. Frequency told CamShaft to execute the light it up scenario. The ship became translucent and the sea animals could see inside. Frequency went to the side of the ship and touched it. The big whale put his eye directly on the spot where Frequency hand was. After Grounds saw that, he told Kahuna, that they would be crazy not the let this guy join them. Kahuna laughed as all the crew was looking in amazement. Frequency then told the crew that they were aboard the CyberEye hybrid yacht. He also explained that it was mixed with a sub and hydrofoil. He explained that it is a very fast and elusive ship with all the amenities of a modern-day luxury liner. CyberEye has the capabilities of every water-based vehicle made available to a modern navy. Frequency told Eyeball he would come out for a swim later and that they did a great job of keeping the ship hidden while he was away.

Thumpf was notified of the escape and he was furious. He grabbed the briefcase and beat it against the wall and then kicked it down the hall. It flew across the blue threshold and activated all the intel inside. Thumpf decided to take matters in his own hands and release another set of viruses to teach those, who defy him. And this time it will not discriminate.

Broke the #1 Rule

The hospitals were overwhelmed at an alarming rate. This new strain of the virus mainly affected the women and children. Thumpf announced to America that it was all a hoax, and this was a ploy just to get everyone riled up over the last election. After each city started pleading for supplies, Thumpf sent in the military to handle all the day to day activities of each major city.

Thumpf had each of his older family members running the manufacturing processes and then sell them to the USA at a higher rate.

The Thumpf family was raking in millions of dollars daily as the USA suffered through this virus epidemic.

Thumpf then had MaHoodi send out propaganda videos to keep the USA at odds with him and his terrorist regime, all the while profiting through outside means from the Thumpf family.

Kahuna was in hiding on the CyberEye. He was getting his information from certain news agencies. But every time one of them talked against the Thumpf family something would take them off the air. Most of it was virus related but targeted to down that news source.

LabRat was using everything he had been taught to keep from getting caught. He had found out that the Thumpf family had been planning the coup day one Thumpf was sworn in as President. Now LabRat needed a way to get himself sent home so that he could let the outside know what he had learn. LabRat knew he couldn't take the inaugural briefcase out of the White House because it would sound all kinds of alarms and would have him caught up in all kinds of trouble. LabRat was called by the Secret Service Detail Commander. He needed LabRat to go down into an old staff elevator shaft to pull the inaugural briefcase out of it. Thumpf in one of his tantrums Kicked the briefcase and it felled down into the shaft. They called LabRat because he was small enough to go down into the shaft without getting stuck. LabRat agreed to go get the briefcase and he went and got the equipment needed to do the job. He had a couple of senior Agents to help him just in case, something went wrong. LabRat repelled down the shaft with no problem. They used flashlight as signals so because the shaft was so old and had no power to it. LabRat got the case and noticed that it had been activated so how. This was perfect and now the only thing LabRat had to do is notify the right crew.

Thumpf was just finishing up his plans to go play golf. He told his Secretary of State to make sure all the other people's family got the virus and take them to the special holding center for treatment.

The family and friends were attacked in their homes, on the street, in the movie theaters, and in church. The crew sprayed the virus directly on the women and children then escorted them away. Grounds was the 1st to get notified, Fly was 2nd and then Kahuna. The crew was surprised that Bhang was so calm then he told them his big secret. He told them that He and Victoria had gotten married and decided to keep it a secret. The crew was shocked and then angered, when Frequency intercepted a communication that the VP elect had been infected by the virus and taken to an undisclosed location designated by Thumpf.

The crew immediately went and prepared themselves to go get their families. They gotten dressed into the Kriss Assault system but was stopped by Frequency. Frequency asked the crew did they know where the women were being kept. No, then he asked how many guards or soldiers in place. Kahuna had to calm himself and tell his crew to stand down. They all agreed and then Frequency asked if he could join their crew and help bring this mess to an end. The crew agreed and then Frequency had them follow him to the Assault room. Here they started to put together a plan to rescue their families.

LabRat finally got the case tied off and he sent the case back up the shaft. The two senior Agents grabbed the case and left LabRat to climb out on his own. LabRat figured they would do something like this, because they were always pranking the jr agents. LabRat was climbing up and found something that could help him get the message out. It was an old flip phone. It was low on battery, but it worked. LabRat sent out a simple text that would notify the one person, who could help him out of the White House.

Agents Masters and Layrock both got a text and immediately headed for the White House. Their special clearance gave them access to the Secret Service commander and he basically couldn't stop them. The two agents got into the White House and asked the commander for Agent Ratcliffe. He told them that LabRat was receiving an item for the Red Commander and he should have been back by now. The three men went to the area where they were supposed to be working but no one was there. All the equipment was there but no agents. Layrock looked down into the shaft and saw a dim light. He plugged in the winch and started pulling up whatever was attached to it. As it got to the top the agents saw LabRat hanging on barely and he was out of it. Agent Master helped Layrock get LabRat out of the shaft and they were both hit with a toxic smell that kind of overwhelmed them all. The Commander immediately got a maintenance crew on scene to find out what was the cause, get it fixed before it caused any more damage, and insure that it was not flammable. Master and LayRock told the Commander that they would get LabRat to hospital facility for observation and then, they would be back in contact with him. The commander approved it and they all got busy to fix this issue.

As soon as They got to the car Layrock put an oxygen mask on LabRat. He and Master hurriedly got away from the grid observation of the White House before they began talking. Mack Master pulled the oxygen mask away from LabRat and he began telling them everything that he had learned. LayRock was upset but he knows had to try something he had not used in years.

LayRock pulled out his cell phone and called a number that was attached to the Child Abatement Team. As soon as the recording tone beeped LayRock stated Frequency Hunter, then hung up. LabRat thought to himself that no one had heard from him in years, why now.

Layrock knew it was a long shot, but there was no way that any other organization could battle Thumpf and not be taken down by the Secret Service.

Mack Master was headed to a spot where they could hide out, when all of a sudden his GPS came online and pointed them to the shoreline.

The three agents made it to the shoreline and was met with a sight for sore eyes. It was a fully healed Frequency Hunter and he was ready to take on the Thumpf Regime. They all were hugging and happy, but they had to get on the CyberEye quickly. As soon as they got onboard, Frequency introduced them to the Pantha Pack crew. Frequency then told the crew that LabRat was the inside at the White House that led them to him. The crew thanked LabRat and then LabRat told them that somehow Thumpf staff had activated the inaugural briefcase, kind of making Kahuna the President. Bhang asked LabRat what that means. LabRat explained that because they activated the case, we now have two presidents. Thumpf and the new President Elect. LabRat then gave them the bad news. He told them that Thumpf had released another virus and had snatched all their family members. He pulled out a hard drive and gave it to Frequency. The drive had the layout to all the government secret holding facilities.

Frequency had CyberEye search for the all the hostages and it did not take long to find them. The problem was it was more than they had anticipated. CyberEye then notified Frequency that the whales where trying to send a message. Frequency told CyberEye to translate and it was a bold plan to get all the hostages in one big swoop.

Frequency shared the ideal with the crew and they were all in. Frequency then took the guys into the assault shop so that DocBot could get them ready for a serious extraction. That would teach Thumpf the consequences of not to break the

#1 rule of never hurting women and children.

Never dead, always Upgraded

The plan came together rather quickly once Frequency had entered the info from LabRat hard drive. The crew was getting retrofitted with all the latest tech gear that Frequency had designed for this mission. Each member was fitted with a rebreather and propellers. No one had to worry about weapons because everything had been integrated into their nano-suits. The hostages would be placed into a glass container that could withstand armor piercing rounds and was totally self-contained once it was in the water. Frequency had Fly take on the Airfish with its new kinetic munition system. Fly was like a kid in a candy store. And before he could take off, Kahuna told him he couldn't get one of those, because it was only one. Fly laughed and went got comfortable in the pilot seat of the AirFish. Next, Bhang and Grounds both had sea breachers to get familiar with. After a couple of tests, they had it down to a science. Kahuna was watching and taking notes, when Frequency had a big knock on the front door for him. It was a Cyber truck loaded down with heavy munitions. Kahuna main assignment was to take out as many of the Metal Storm gun Array systems, and if possible, capture a major player in Thumpf's organization.

Kahuna looked at the truck and had one question, did he have to return it unscratched. Frequency was hoping not to see it again because he kind of borrowed the design. The two men laughed and got ready for the rescue. Kahuna then went out and got into the AirFish with Fly and they took off the drop point.

Doorshaker had a simple delivery sheet. Go to wharf with delivery sheet. They would load container onto goose neck trailer. Deliver to address on paper, call number on sheet with routing

number. Get paid in full. You couldn't
ask for an easier delivery in such hard
times. Doorshaker followed
instructions and immediately noticed
that the crate was not strapped
down. He was about to go strap
down the load but then he saw the
load lock itself to the goose neck.
Now this would have had anyone
else thinking they were gone crazy,
but Doorshaker had loaded stuff that
would make a praying man burn his
bible. The driver got the package
loaded and immediately headed for
the destination.

It doesn't take him long to get
to the address of the package drop
off. The instruction stated for the

driver to do a hard-left turn and wait
for the final instructions. Doorshaker
followed instructions and as he made
the hard circle turn the package
came off of the goose neck trailer
and landed perfectly in the park spot.
Doorshaker was about to go check on
load when a voice came across the
radio and told him job well done, call
to collect your pay. No question
asked Doorshaker made the call and
then check the transfer to see if he
was paid. The amount was double
the negotiated rate and Doorshaker
was headed to the yard paid and
happy.

CamShaft and Kahuna were dropped in front of the crate and immediately broke down the crate. The vehicle inside of it was all that Frequency had described. One push of a button and Kahuna was headed to the front door of the place, where all the hostages were being held. Kahuna had in the back of his mind that he was now the President of the USA, but then these people had his wife and loved one held hostage. Make it good because it would be a while before you would be able to do this every again.

Docbot loaded the Devil Dawgs
with a gas propelled antiserum
solution. All four dawgs had enough
to get everybody healed as soon as
they breathe in the solution. The
assault team was ready and waiting
for the knock on the door. Kahuna
said a quick prayer and then he
activated the system and blew the
entry gate wide open. The big truck
responded like it looked. As fast as
Kahuna saw something as a threat
the truck fired one of its many
munition systems to get rid of it.
Camshaft notified Kahuna of all the
Metal Storm systems and they
started to take them down. Things
were going good on top for Kahuna

he prayed the same was going good underwater.

Bhang was releasing the fluids into the water as he was designated. He and Grounds was trying to figure out how this fluid would open this giant watertight door. Grounds was enjoying the deep sea breacher and he was making designs in the ocean. He decided to make one of an whale and then they were notified that they had some big company headed their way and it was coming fast.

Frequency told Bhang and Grounds to dump all the fluids at the door and then get out of there fast. Both men followed instructions and then they were witness to something only heard of in old sea tales. The biggest whale they have ever seen rammed headfirst into the watertight doors. The ground underneath collapsed instantly as the 100 plus ton mammal slammed his full girth on to the building's water landing. Frequency called out to the crew and introduced them to Bully, the lead whale of Eyeball's pack. Fly was in awe as the big whale breached the surface to exert his dominance over anything trying to move into his territory. Bully moved around quickly and hit the building one more time collapsing the infrastructure deep under water.

Bhang and Grounds immediately moved inside the building and started preparing the area for the hostages. Kahuna made it to his drop area and released the Devil Dawgs. The Dawgs went in and dropped soldier's dead as they made it into the A/C system of the facility. The Dawgs released the 1st half of the antiserum into the A/C system and then they went to free the hostages. CamShaft was dropped off at the main control center. He was able to gain control easily and open all the doors to release the hostages.

The Ladies were the 1st to notice that they were not feeling sick and sluggish anymore. They immediately notice that the guards were hollering and running scared. Blood burst from one of the guards as this little 2 minigun firing robot was mowing them down. The women were confused until Victoria heard a voice that she had been longing to hear. Bhang hugged his wife and told her to get all the hostages ready to get out of here. Victoria grabbed his hand and took him into a room that had hundreds of missing and exploited children in it. Grounds walked up behind them and saw the same picture.

Grounds immediately called out to Frequency and asked him how they were going to help all these children. Frequency then told the crew that he kind of over did the water containers. The Devil Dawgs pulled the 1st container in and quickly assembled it. The 1st batch of children got in and were pushed into the flood zone. The Dawgs did these three more times and it was enough room for everybody to get out of the hostage area.

No was left behind as Kahuna finally found the Metal Storm Control Center. Kahuna drove the truck directly into the center killing all the people that were running it.

The Secretary of Defense had no place to go. This big offense took out everything they could throw at it and now they were at a loss. Kahuna saw the Secretary and easily knocked him out and captured him. Kahuna carried him to the wet drop and noticed all the holding cells these people had made. Kahuna turned a corner short bumping the Secretary of Defense hard against the door jam. He finally made it to the container, and he put the Officer inside. He quickly went and grabbed his wife. He kissed and hugged her tight but had to let go because they had to get them out of there before the big explosion.

Everybody was gone except Kahuna and the Devil Dawgs, Kahuna said to the them, hope you can swim as he dived into the water and started his journey out of this hell hole. The Devil Dawgs converted to water mode and moved through the water with their converted fins.

Frequency was given the all the clear and he gave Fly full firing authorization of the AirFish to start annihilating the hostage compound. Immediately, the 1st pulse missile hit the electrical grid, then communications, then main gas line. The Assault truck self-destructed and shutdown the entire Metal Storm grid Array. The building collapsed into the sea as the hostages were in the safety of the see-through containers. Bhang and Grounds were just as amazed because Frequency had Beluga whales pulling the hostages to safety and to keep anybody from coming up from behind, Eyeball the whale had it covered. The Devil Dawgs connected as one and had Kahuna riding on top as they headed for the CyberEye.

Thumpf was notified that he had lost all the hostages, destroyed the Metal Storm plus they had the Secretary of Defense. Thumpf was infuriated and immediately had all available law enforcement go and search all their homes. Thumpf told his staff to turn over ever rock until they found, whoever was responsible for this. They went to all the women homes and tore it apart. The men hurt their pets and left them for dead. They pushed people around, but they had nothing because the people they were looking for had totally vanished. The news got back to Thumpf and he knew he was in a serious pickle, if he didn't get his staff member back. He made the call to all of his black-market cohorts and he gave them open reigns to find out, who destroyed his hostage compound.

Frequency intercepted communications about the ransacking of the pack's homes. He immediately dispatched the Devil Dawgs to each of the members houses and stop them dead from damaging the properties. The Dawgs split up and took care of the people, who were in each of the Packs houses. The Dawgs had to rescue all their pets because they got injured while defending their territories. The Devil Dawgs made short work of the humans and then made haste to get the injured pets to DocBot so that she could get them back up on their feet in no time.

Kahuna, Fly, Bhang and Grounds were distraught, when they got the news that their homes were ransacked and their pets were injured severely. The women went into the triage area and were amazed at how super advanced the setup was on the ship. DocBot stepped into the area and they started talking about the animals and all their work that was rescued by the Devil Dawgs. Lady Kahuna asked Frequency could they be allowed to interact with DocBot to come up with a permanent solution to some of the stuff that was being used on them. As soon as they were given permission Lady Grounds pulled her data for the use of herbs and they all used it and other details from Lady Fly to come up with a strong antitoxin that could help the body's immune system fight off these viruses as soon as it is introduced.

The crew came in and saw their pets in the incubation tanks. Fly stated that they looked as if they were dead. And CamShaft stated "Never Dead, Always Upgraded"!

On Board CyberEye (formerly the Lotus Blossom sub/yacht

Frequency Hunter sat back and watched all the rescued people enjoy freedom at his expense. He took them all out to an island that was uninhabited and cleaned them up. DocBot made sure everyone had was fitted with universal translators so that they could communicate openly. Frequency used his closed network and had clothes and hygiene products droned in from various connection that were in the vicinity. He also had them put on high alert about the calamity coming from the powers that be. The Kahunas were cooking as if they were home in Hawaii during a time of celebration. All the food was either gather from the island or either droned in to make sure the meal was extra special. The Fly family had sneaked off to have a little mountain time to themselves. Fly was crazy about his wife and soon as he was about to kiss her again, they were interrupted by their baby Feathers. The big sea eagle dropped in so elegantly that both Mr. and Mrs. had to give their pet a big hug. Feathers then started moving his legs so that they would notice the watches on them. Fly took the watches off Feathers and looked at it. The screen lit up and instructed him and his wife put them on and follow the guide. The two of them did as instructed and to their amazement they were able to communicate with Feathers effortlessly. Fly had a mode in which he could see what Feathers see as he flew around. For giggles, Fly told Feathers to spread his wings. The big eagle spread his massive wings fully and without any pain. Fly hugged his big bird and then he was hit with the message that he was hungry, and Kahuna was cooking a feast for a king. The Fly family laughed and then headed for the cookout.

Grounds and Mrs. were sitting in a small lava pool when Diggs took them their watches. They followed instructions and were soon loving on their pet as he told them that dinner was ready. The Grounds got dressed and headed to the dinner that Kahuna had laid out. The Bhangs were up in a tree making up for lost time. Bhang was not going to let his woman tap him out after all the time they had been apart. Victoria was just happy to be back in the arms of her protector and she was not taking no for an answer. They were laying in one another arms when they heard a low growl. As Bhang raised his hands Claws jumped into his grasp. They hugged the big cat and saw the watches attached to its collar. They took them off and followed instructions. They were now able to communicate with Claws and were instructed to come on in for the big Feast that Kahuna had prepared. They jumped from the tree into the beautiful water and then headed to the awaiting feast.

Kahuna was overjoyed to see everyone enjoying the meal. He felt something touching on his ankle and it was his pal Slick. The sea lion ran into Kahuna's leg and was hugging onto the big man's thigh. Frequency had given him and the Mrs. their watches earlier. Kahuna loved being able to communicate with Slick.

What he didn't like was how someone hurt him while they were ransacking their home. Kahuna laughed when Slick messaged him about how the Devil Dawg rescued him and took care of business with those humans so that they would not be hurting anything else.

Everyone arrived in time for a great prayer and feast fit for a king's court for years to come. But after the meal everyone had on their minds, what happens now that all of them were on the run. Frequency told them to enjoy the meal for now, and we will make a way in the morning.

The nights rest was interrupted by the movement of the ship. Frequency put the ship in transparent mode and saw blood in the water. Frequency immediately put on a rebreather and dove into the water. One of the beluga whales swam close to Frequency and took him over to the injured whale laying on the dune. It was Eyeball's mom. She had been hit by a couple of whaler's harpoons. The cables had been cut but the harpoons were stuck deep into the whale fin and side. Before Frequency could react, the Ladies were there to help him heal the whale. The ladies had DocBot running a simulation within their helmets, so that they knew exactly what to do to save the

mother whale. Frequency had
CamShaft take the harpoons and
make a couple of box loads of
harpoon heads out of them. As soon
as the ladies told Frequency that the
momma whale was going to be
alright, he went back to the ship to
get revenge.

Fly was amazed at how his wife
and others quickly jumped in to save
the whale. Frequency called Fly and
asked him to help him load the boxes
of harpoon heads onto the AirFish.
Frequency asked Fly was he up for
some nighttime flight ops. Fly was
eager and ready. They Airfish was
airborne in full stealth mode.
Frequency had Fly take him over the

whaling ship first and then to an old acquaintance that would love to extend some equal justice to these whalers.

WhiteFace and Mrs. Baton was on the 28th floor enjoying the night air of the balcony. They were saying their goodbyes when they were interrupted by a voice that was familiar, but they haven't heard of in years. WhiteFace went for a weapon but couldn't move. Mrs. Baton was in the same predicament, so they stopped struggling and started talking. Frequency stepped from the AirFish and onto the balcony. He asked them to listen to his proposal and if they agreed, he would ensure that they were well compensated for it. They both agreed and Frequency shutdown the emp emitter and had the robots unload a package at WhiteFace's feet. WhiteFace opened the box and it was filled with his custom cut harpoon heads. Mrs. Baton immediately asked, what did he need to do? Frequency told them both about the illegal whaling ship that was also exporting exploited children. He told WhiteFace that he had nothing to stop him from laying out his judge, jury , executioner type justice but he needed to get Mrs. Baton the proof she needed to shutdown the companies and make them pay for hurting the animals and children. Mrs. Baton agreed and

WhiteFace asked Frequency, how would he get out to the whaling ship. Frequency gave him watch and told him to notify him via the watch.

Frequency told them to enjoy the rest of their night as he walked and jumped off the balcony. The two watched in amazement as Fly easily caught him out of the air and flew away silently. Mrs. Baton went and grabbed a hidden camera she had stashed in the room. WhiteFace asked her was she videoing them having sex. She said of course, there was no way she was trying not to have proof of this amazing sex they were having. WhiteFace looked at her and said "REALLY". Mrs. Baton didn't resist as he took the camera from her and decided to make another video before taking care of Frequency's request.

Just before daybreak, WhiteFace was dropped out to the ship. Frequency Hunter was a man with plenty of tech to get him out to the ship totally undetected. WhiteFace moved around the ship and got proof of the illegal fishing and whaling activities. Then he was about to go for the children, when one of the guys came in with a human torso. They had harvested everything that they could from it and now preparing it for bait. The man called out to the ship's mechanic and asked, how much longer before the ship would be running. He was told that the last Whale rapped the cables into the screws, and it would be another four hours before they could get back to running. That's all that WhiteFace needed to hear. The ship hand was harpooned to the wall. Whiteface moved quickly administering justice throughout the interior of the ship. A few of the men put up a fight but useless. WhiteFace was taking no prisoners. He made to the holding cells and there he found the children. They were malnourished but alive.

WhiteFace contacted Mrs. Baton and she did the rest. She and the coast guard boarded the ship to see the blood bath but rescue all the children that were onboard. They even found video of how ship's company was harvesting the organs of the children then using the torsos for bait of the illegal fishing activities.

Mrs. Baton had cameras, cops, and coast guard out on the ship to well document all of the illegal acts. She knew this was a big thing and had to get prepared for the repercussions that was going to follow. WhiteFace shook hands with Frequency and the two men agreed to stay in contact, when it came down to the business of rescuing children. Frequency then gave WhiteFace a message that would link them for life. He told WhiteFace that he would serve his brother's killers to him an Olympic style platter soon. WhiteFace told Frequency that he would be looking forward to it.

Frequency quickly headed back to the CyberEye. He was met by Mrs. Fly and she told him that the whale was doing great and would recover with no problems. Frequency thanked her and went on to get some food because the night had taking a toll on his stomach.

Fly shutdown the AirFish and went to spend some time with his wife. The night had made a true believer in him and now they all had to rest, because they all had become a part of the family onboard of the CyberEye. And now they had to work to take back all the wrongs issued in by Thumpf.

K.O. KnockOut

The antidote that Frequency used on the hostages worked. It was totally experimental and now he needed more to get it out to all the victims of the virus. Frequency gathered the crew and told them where he got the ideal for the antidote. Bad part was that he used all he had to save the hostages. Frequency told the crew that he would need all their help to gather all of the ingredients to make more antiserum, but it wasn't going to be easy.

Everybody was onboard, and immediately began working on the list of ingredients. Everything was going flawlessly until they got to the last thing on the list and it was a major one. They needed a plant called blood weed and it was plenty on one farm that would take some strong negotiations to get.

KnockOut Ranch was a legal marijuana farm owned by one of the greatest boxing champs of the world. Since his retirement he had greatly prospered on the legalization of marijuana. He had several specialty strands of plant, but his most exotic was called blood weed. This weed grew under a vampire bat cave and was totally sustained by the bats. All the grower had to do was wait till the bats finished feeding off of the stalk of the plants and harvest all of the buds. Lately, the bats had become larger and more aggressive, so the champ had to secure the weed in its on environment to keep everything safe from the bats more aggressive feeding habit.

The whole crew flew out to the ranch to talk to the champ. They all explained everything to him to try and convince him to give them that last ingredient. The champ told them how aggressive the bats have become, and they would be on their own, simply because he was afraid of bats. Bhang didn't laugh because he didn't like them either. The others were all laughing till the big bats dropped down and grabbed up one of the midsize plants and feasted on it. What they saw was truly amazing. The plant emitted a blood like fluid that dripped down on the ground and fertilized the new growth. The vampire bats feasted on this fluid and it totally curved their need for actual blood. The champ asked the crew who was going inside to get the buds off the ground. All the women were inside of the gate before the champ could warn them about the bats. The women were inside working and one of them hooked themselves on a shard of metal. The lead bat sensed blood and was on the ground to investigate the source. Lady Grounds tried to cover up, but the big bat was on her quickly. Before it could strike it shrieked and went back up deep into the cave. CamShaft had started to use sonar to interrupt the bats senses. The big bat flew away giving the women enough time to get all that they needed plus a whole blood weed plant to cultivate for future use.

The champ was impressed but was not willing to give up one of his cash crops plants. Frequency and Kahuna immediately went into negotiations with him to come up with some type of mutual agreement. The champ didn't need money or business connect, what he wanted was CamShaft. Frequency could not give CamShaft away, if he wanted too. That was Teez guard and only she could give CamShaft away.

The negotiations were spiraling fast and neither side was willing to budge until Bhang notices an old metal padded practice stand. Bhang pulled Frequency to the side and asked him, if he could make the Champ his very own CamShaft. Bhang then pointed to the old punching stand and Frequency smiled.

Frequency asked the Champ about the old punching stand and the Champ stated that the stand had been with him from the beginning of his boxing career. He stated that the stand would be a permanent part of his life until the end. Frequency then asked the Champ if he would agree to allow him to make the stand into his very own guardian. The Champ loved the ideal and told Frequency if he did that, he could have anything he needed. The two men shook hands and Frequency had the stand and the Champ join him on the AirFish for a ride out to the CyberEye. The women stayed behind to get the antiserum made up so that they could be ready to move against the Thumpf regime.

The Champ was in awe of the CyberEye. He loved how DocBot took the stand and him to integrate his ideals into his own guard bot. Once the data was gathered and secured the process began and the Champ was informed of all the chaos that had befallen them. As soon as he heard about the exploited children, he wanted in on the assault. Frequency told the Champ about the President and the Champ gave him everything he needed to know. The Champ and Thumpf had done business before and Thumpf like to brag about his doomsday scenario bunker, that was located on his private island next to the Hawaii peninsula. Kahuna laughed and stated that he knew about that project but couldn't stop them because it was totally private funded. He laughed because it was built on a newly active Volcano vein.

Frequency now had the piece of the puzzle he needed to bring down Thumpf. He immediately started working with the crew to ensure they could pull it off without a hitch. DocBot interrupted the men and informed them that the Devil Dawgs were escorting the new guard bot called KO to the KnockOut ranch. The Champ thanked everybody and then

Frequency decided to give the Champ one more surprise. He told CyberEye to go into transparent mode and introduced the Champ to his underwater friends. The Champ was ecstatic and promised Frequency he would be there for him, when he needed him.

The Champ was taken back to the ranch and KO was programmed to him. They all then were boarded back onto CyberEye to begin the quest to regain control of the White House.

Volcano

Feathers flew low into the heart of the epicenter releasing thousands of micro nanobots into the atmosphere. Each nanobot carried the new antiserum that the women had created. The big bird flew into the area unopposed by any of the Secret Service detection systems. Feathers made several passes into the heart of the areas mostly infected. Meanwhile, Diggs had found a burrow that led him to an underground well that fed directly into the city's water system. Diggs released the thousands of nanobots into the water system to release antiserum into it also. Claws was on a mission to find Teez and notify her that help was on the way. As soon as he would be seen by someone on the outside, they would scream in fear of the big cat. Claws would evade capture and would release nanobots to help with getting the antiserum out into the public. Slick was in his zone as he had recruited hundreds of sea lions to carry antiserum filled bubbles and release them into the water treatment plant. The plant was offline by design because the big sea lions had overwhelmed the flood gate. Slick and his bunch then release the bubbles into the water system and decided to sunbathe on the open dock plate.

The crew had already notified Baton and WhiteFace about the missing children and they had provided a place for them to be safe. One of the exploited children told WhiteFace that Ms. Bobbi had issued a hit out on the Baton. WhiteFace checked into his sources and sure enough there was a million-dollar bounty on the Baton. WhiteFace was furious and he decided that as soon as he made sure these children and the Baton was safe. He would make an example out of Ms. Bobbi and her cronies.

Frequency had managed to get LabRat back into the White House undetected. He told LabRat to get ready with all the agents not loyal to Thumpf and to provide them with the information they needed to bring this coup to an end. LabRat thanked Frequency for not being dead and Frequency promised him to not to come up missing again. Next Frequency needed to know how the fight against the virus was going. He needed someone on the inside and then he had an idea. He knew he just couldn't show up at hospitals and started asking questions, but he knew of just the right person to handle this mission.

The Champ had started his day going from hospital to hospital visiting sick patients. He made his way through each one signing autographs and taking pictures. He went through several makeshift hospitals until he got to this peculiar one in the heart of the epicenter. This setup had guards and some of them were heavily armed. The Champ was unbothered and went through to greet the sick people, who were trying to recover from the virus. As the Champ made his way through this one unit a handful of guards confronted him about his movements. The big foreign accent man stood in challenge of the Champ's movement and was met with resistance immediately. As the shoving and shouting were starting to break out into a full-blown brawl, one lady walked in between the two men and got them to settle down. She immediately got the Champ on to a different area from the guard. The Champ was still ready to throw hands with the big guard, when he heard the lady ask him about his lapel pin. The Champ told this new friend of his, had it made for him and it was supposed to be his guardian. The lady saw the eyes of the pin turn purple and she told the Champ that he should tell his friend thanks for making a very interesting jewelry piece. The Champ then asked the lady her name, and she said my friends call me Teez.

The Thumpf family was on the move. All his plans were coming unraveled as fast as he came up with them. His secretary of defense had been captured or killed. And his Metal Storm Array control center had been destroyed. The only thing was going well was the release of the virus and the havoc of Abu MaHoodi. Thumpf was being notified of the whereabouts of all his people and how soon that they would be in his big bunker safe house. Thumpf's children had been scaling up their personal wealth and connections. They were shocked when they're personal security teams came in and whisked them away to the private bunker. All the security teams were checking in except two of them. Telsa and Bernhard Thumpf were not cooperating with their security staff. Thumpf got so upset at Telsa that he told the head of her security to hit her with a stun gun, if he had to. Telsa was not having it. She was working on a new project and her dad being the President had become a big inconvenience. Telsa locked herself into a room at modeling agency, that her mom owned. She thought she could wait it out, but the security team picked the lock and hit her with a stun gun. When she came to, she was on her way to the bunker whether she liked it or not.

Bernhard was totally in his own zone, playing laser tag within a secure closed system. He was totally caught off guard, when the place was stormed by the Secret Service and he was escorted out of the place quickly. Bernhard laughed as he saw Telsa looking as if she been dancing under an electrode. Telsa wanted to hit her little brother but she was still woozy from the stun gun. She would wait till they got to their destination and then she and her dad was going to have it out once and for all.

The 1st Lady Thumpf was all settled into the bunker, she had known about it for years and made sure that it had all of the comfort that she desired. As more of the family arrived Mrs. Thumpf showed them to their personal suites and made sure they understood that she was the grand hostess of the secure facility. As the last of the family and administration arrived Thumpf had the facility put in full locked down mode. He had ensured that the facility was setup with all of the survival gear and the American tax dollar paid for it.

Thumpf then contacted Abu MaHoodi and told him that he could start the invasion as soon as he was ready. Abu MaHoodi acknowledged

Thumpf and went on the offensive. Abu MaHoodi had all his troops loaded into trucks and head into the island area where he had been smuggling them in. Feathers sounded the alarm and the Pantha Pack immediately started attacking the convoy with an aerial attack. The big eagle was the eyes, but Fly was the arsenal. He used the kinetic rector pulse system to take out the convoy with ease. Bhang and Grounds were on the assault taking out the lead and rear trucks , so that there was no retreat.

Abu MaHoodi received the message that his convoy had been ambushed and destroyed. He immediately dispatched his whole undercover army to destroy the infidels and to take over their country. Abu MaHoodi saw that he totally underestimated his opponent. Kahuna had gathered all the military forces and they were fighting mad that this terrorist had invaded their home and was trying to take over. The battle for the island had commenced and both opponents threw their best into the battle.

Thumpf had the big bunker's environmental system fired up but what he didn't anticipate was that the heat exhaust from the system was being fed directly to an exhaust port of an active Volcano. The more

the system worked the more
unstable the Volcano became until it
erupted. Thumpf and everyone inside
knew they had sealed their doom.
The big doors and evacuation system
had been fried when a lava ball was
blown into it. Everyone inside the
bunker immediately started
panicking and screaming, Thumpf got
on the emergency phone and
contacted the White House for help.

LabRat and the agents were
cleaning up the mess in the White
House. The rogue agents decided to
fight instead of run. All hands-on
deck was either battling for the old
president or the new one. The lead
Agent received Thumpf's distress call

and put in a beacon of distress to all military entities. As soon as they finished taking care of the terrorist the Thumpf family was next. Kahuna had made his way into the control center of Abu MaHoodi. He, Bhang, and Grounds were kicking ass and not taking names. They had to capture Abu MaHoodi and they had to keep him alive. Abu MaHoodi had his crimson guard by his side, and he felt invincible. Abu MaHoodi was arrogant and wealthy thanks to his brother's wealth. He had been learning military tactics and hand to hand combat technics, while studying abroad. He would have to put it all into play to make this plan work and so far, his military tactics were failing.

His crimson army couldn't handle the American joined forces. He and his guards were about leave the command post, when the Pantha Pack came in and started battling with them. The guards ran out of ammo immediately and the crew decided to put their hand to hand skills to the test. Kahuna took on Abu MaHoodi and left the rest to Bhang and Grounds. Bhang took out two of the guards with ease, the last one took a little skill and blade play to end his life.

Grounds had busted up his guard's limbs and left his combat knife protruding out of the last one eye socket. Kahuna told Abu

MaHoodi that he was not going to let him die and get all those virgins he was promised. Kahuna stated that Abu MaHoodi should get used to living behind bars being experimented on. Abu MaHoodi attacked Kahuna and the two men battled for a solid ten minutes before Abu MaHoodi sliced Kahuna with sword. Kahuna flinched gained his composure then caught Abu MaHoodi slipping by stomping his foot and then hitting him with a jaw breaking uppercut that left him knocked unconscious.

The epicenter was abuzz with activity. A lot of the patients started showing signs of recovery from the virus. Frequency was happy that he was able to help so many people afflicted by this virus. Before Frequency could enjoy his accomplishment, he overheard a voice over the radio that sent a chill through his spine. One of the guards was ease dropping on the Champ, when Teez told him her name. Ms. Bobbi had a reward for anybody that could tell her where Teez was. The guard immediately got in touch with Ms. Bobbi peeps and they told him that they would be there shortly. The guard loaded his weapon and was ready to do whatever it took to collect that reward money.

Ms. Bobbi arrived with a small army being loud, proud and obnoxious. Where that bitch at? Teez, you can't hide from bitch. Save me the trouble of looking for you, because it's not going to be a good look. Frequency broke protocol and immediately headed for the epicenter. He used a prototype ejector wing setup to gain flight. He then used a squirrel suit to glide into the epicenter and landed undetected. Frequency had one plan and one plan only. Protect Teez at all cost. Frequency slipped into the hospital's security room and asset the situation. The Champ was about to leave the center, when his lapel pin started vibrating. The Champ touched the pin and Frequency immediately told the Champ that the nurse he met was about to be assaulted by a gang. The Champ told Frequency that he was on it and he went back into the epicenter looking for Teez. Teez was helping a sick patient when a guard grabbed her from behind. Teez made short work of dude and finished taking care of the patient. Teez left the patient's room and heard fighting in the upper lobby, before she could make it up there the Champ knocked out the big guard and came running to her. The Champ told Teez that some big mouth woman was screaming for her and she had a army with her. Teez told the Champ that Ms. Bobbi was no woman and her army was the saggyboi club gangsters. The Champ said, wait a minute, they all that LGBTWxyz community. Teez laughed and told him yes. The Champ tapped his lapel and told Frequency that he had Teez. Frequency told them, where to go to hide, he was coming and bringing the calvary.

Frequency alerted the crew about what was going on in the epicenter. He told them to make sure they stopped Thumpf and he was calling in the cavalry. Kahuna told Frequency to be careful and let the dawgs loose. Ms. Bobbi thought she had the epicenter under control till she heard men screaming and running. She pulled out her two machine guns and called out for the assassins to cover her back.

What they saw next was totally unsettling. This big robotic dog had one of her bois in his mouth and he split him in two. They immediately started firing their weapons. Bronze found them a way out and the four ladies hurriedly found their Lincoln SUV and they took off with their convoy in tow. Frequency found the Champ and Teez. He gave the Champ a handshake and hug for being there for him. He then turned to Teez and she gave him the biggest hug and kiss. Frequency had to remind himself that they were in the middle of a battle, so he pulled himself away from Teez and immediately changed out her earrings for something that was more befitting. Frequency then told Teez to call him. Teez called out to CamShaft and her little guard showed up to get on his job. CamShaft came out of the sewer system and he had the Devil Dawgs with him for backup. They shut down the rift at the epicenter and was by Frequency side to await pickup. Frequency thanked the Champ again and the Champ told him anytime he needed him, just get in contact with him and he would be there. The Champ and his crew left, and

Frequency turned to Teez just to look at her.

Teez reminded Frequency that it has been five years that he had been missing. Frequency motioned to Teez to be quiet and he would explain everything once they got back to CyberEye.

Teez asked Frequency what happened to Lotus Blossom, Frequency told her that was now her area of the ship because of the total new upgrade. Teez had plenty questions but she would wait till they were safe before she got her answers.

The fat lady started to sing as indictments and news media was a buzz with the end of a major coup. Thumpf and his entire family had to be rescued from the impending danger of the erupting Volcano. The Secretary of State was immediately arrested once the aircraft landed on foreign soil. The Secretary of Defense had already begun interrogating with the CIA and his testimony was damning. Kahuna and his crew showed up at the White House with Abu MaHoodi in chains. All the other players involved in the coup was slowly being round up by the authorities.

Frequency walked into the White House and awaited his fate. Teez grabbed his hand in assurance that she would be there with him no matter what the outcome was.

Ms. Bobbi and the assassins were on the move. They had cleared their last hangout of any personal information and was headed to catch a plane out of there. WhiteFace was waiting for the four of them on board the private jet. He decided to make a foreboding statement out of them for historical state. As the plane took off the Ms. Bobbi started humming a familiar tune as the pilot stated that they had leveled off and had clear skies all the way to Brazil.

Ms. Bobbi stopped humming and reached for her gun, but it was too late. WhiteFace spent the sawed-off shotgun around and pulled the trigger on both barrels. Ms. Bobbi tried to move but the damage to her groin area was substantial. Gold was next but the heavy barrel of the shotgun bounced of off Gold's head knocking her out. Bronze grabbed WhiteFace from behind but was hit with so many punches and elbows that the floor of the plane was the best place to take a nap. Silver cocked the barrel on the small caliber pistol and pointed it a WhiteFace. WhiteFace laughed because Silver didn't understand how pressurization on a plane works.

WhiteFace had backed up to the door of the plane and was just going to open it up. But a rang from a silver platter knocked Silver out cold. The pilot of the came up from out of the back of the plane and hit Silver knocking her out cold. The pilot told WhiteFace that he had been notified to turn around and land the plane. WhiteFace asked him how much time that he had. The Pilot told him he could buy him an hour. WhiteFace said that would be all the time he needed.

As the plane landed onto the runway it was directed to a private hanger full of government agents. They stormed the plane and where met with a very unsettling sight. All of Ms. Bobbi crew was hung upside down naked from the waist down. Silver had a solid silver cast melted over her groin area. Gold had the same, but it was made of gold and Bronze was made up of bronze. The smelters were still glowing hot as they found a belligerent Ms. Bobbi holding her entrails with a bloody gauge. Her entire groin area had been blown away by the shotgun blast. The agents got the proper medical team into the plane because they had strict instructions no one dies today.

The pilot was questioned, and he told them exactly what he saw when he heard the gun shots. The agents found WhiteFace mask at the rear of the plane, so they knew he had gotten away. WhiteFace really enjoyed flying in the squirrel suit that Frequency had gave him. He had strict instructions not to move once he landed and he would be transported out of the area. As the vehicle pulled up Whiteface pulled out one of his spare cloth masks and entered the vehicle. WhiteFace was immediately paid for the apprehension of Ms. Bobbi and her assassins. He was also paid for finding the stolen gold, silver and bronze bars from the late senator's home. The vehicle stopped at the designated drop where a motorcycle was awaiting WhiteFace. WhiteFace moved quickly he got on the motorcycle and disappeared into the dropping sunset.

The Inauguration of the newly elect President went off without a hitch. Kahuna had his staff in place and insured all his personnel was vetted through his constituency. The new first family move into the White House and immediately began to fix the problems the Thumpf coup had made. President Kahuna enjoyed sitting in on some of the court cases against the Thumpf regime. He laughed at how Ms. Bobbi and her crew was handicapped by the legitimate court system and not one that was bought and paid for via blackmail. All the victims of the viruses were recovering fast and the world was getting back to normal as we know it. Then there was Frequency.

Frequency and Teez sat out on an island with the Devil Dawgs and CamShaft on guard duty. Teez had gotten a briefing from DocBot that answered all her questions concerning Frequency. Teez couldn't stop touching him and holding as if he would just disappear, like a bad dream. Frequency promised her no matter what decision she made; he would always be her friend for life. Teez kissed Frequency and the two enjoyed a private moment until a mist of water showered them. Eyeball's mother showered the two as an expression of gratitude for rescuing her from the harpoon strike. Frequency ran over to touch the mother whale and hug her affectionately. Frequency and Teez then headed back to CyberEye as now they were a part of a special team backed by the President and they worked together to bring an end to child and animal endangerment, cruelty and exploitation.

THE

END

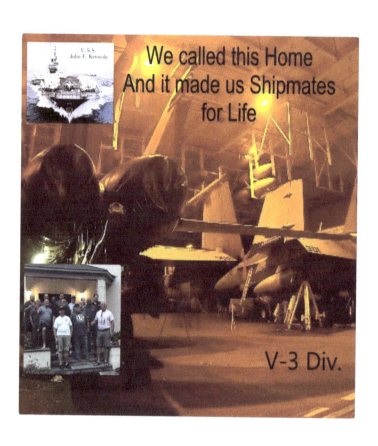

We called this Home
And it made us Shipmates
for Life

U.S.S.
John F. Kennedy

V-3 Div.

F.R.E.A.K.S.

Federal Response Enforcement Against Kid Sex

Ronnie D. Johnson

F.R.E.A.K.S.
FEDERAL RESPONSE ENFORCEMENT AGAINST KID SEX

FREQUENCY HUNTER IS NOT YOUR AVERAGE "JUST RELEASED FROM PRISON" EX CON. No, Hunter has patiently waited for the day he would be free to pursue and take down the rat who betrayed him.

Also a computer genius, there isn't anything Frequency Hunter can.t make a computer do. And after he is released, he realizes that his money worm hack has gone astray and brought him a gift of undeniable sin. Forced to act when he uncovers an underground crime syndicate that thrives on the abuse of children, Hunter reunites with his tried and true comrades, each with their own unique talents, and begins the chase that will either save the lives of innocent children, or cost him and his team their own.

Read the exciting sci-fi thriller
by Ronnie "Ronn Ramm" Johnson
guaranteed to make you ask:

"What If?"

F.R.E.A.K.S. FEDERAL RESPONSE ENFORCEMENT AGAINST KID SEX

RONNIE D. JOHNSON

RONNIE D. JOHNSON

Power source

Camera and microphone

What have your taxes accomplished for YOU!!?

WAR

YOU'VE BEEN FREQ'ED!!

F.R.E.A.K.S. FEDERAL RESPONSE ENFORCEMENT AGAINST KID SEX

When Anarchy Reigns, Frequency Hunter has fully engaged the largest purveyor of filth and now he is battling for his own survival. The billionaire Jahoodi has made his presence known and his only wish is to make anyone connected to Hunter disappear permanently. He has recreated a new team of doctors, scientist, and street pharmacists to create a drug that makes ecstasy seem like Spanish fly.

The entire city is has become the new regimes den of iniquity as the Lickem junkies enjoy the drug of all sex drugs.

Meanwhile a damaged group of friends regroup to get the Nano warriors back online to take down another major syndicate with billions to spend on their destruction.

Read the exciting sci-fi thriller by Ronnie "Ronn Ramm" Johnson, guaranteed to make you say, "You've been Freq'ed !!"

Read the exciting sci-fi thriller
by Ronnie "Ronn Ramm" Johnson
guaranteed to make you ask:
"What If?"

RONNIE D. JOHNSON

RONNIE D. JOHNSON

Character References

Leader D.J. Kahuna (The Rock)

2 Will Fly (Will Smith)

3 Jonathan Bhang (Michael Jai White)

#4 Midas Grounds (Lance Gross)

5 Chad Eyes (TBD)

Vice President Select Victoria Justice (**Simone Missick)** **phD** preventive Medicine

Lady Fly (Roxy Sterberg) phD Veterinarian

1st Lady Select (Grace Park)phD Dermatologist (Mammal)
Lady Grounds (NaFessa Williams) phD Herbologist

Will Fly (pet is rescued Sea Eagle named Feathers)

Bhang (Pet is a rescued Lynk named Claws)
Midas Grounds (Pet is a tough Honey Badger named Diggs)

Kahuna (pet is a sea lion named Slick)

WhiteFace (Westly Snipes)

Bad Team

President Thumpf

Abu MaHoodi

Secretary of Defense

Secretary of State

Thumpf kids

Dolphus Thumpf

Irmina Thumpf

Errol Thumpf

Telsa Thumpf

Bernhard Thumpf

The standing president decide not to admit to defeat,
but start up a hostile coup using a pathogen virus to
turn an election celebration for the winning team into a
chaos and hysteria filled environment.

Bad Team

President Thumpf

Abu MaHoodi

Secretary of Defense

Secretary of State

Will show how a grown up Lab Rat is working for the White House actually foils a plan of the mad crazy President and gives Kahuna a way to bring this craziness to an end.

Synopsis (Ms Bobbi hit squad made up of Trans women , who rape and kill their assignments. Living up to the name assassins)

TSMaddison (MS Bobbi)

ToyaDaBody (Bronze)

ShaunaBrooks (Silver)

SidneyStar (Gold)

This is MS Bobbi last hurrah thanks to the dirt she has on these public officials. She send out the assassins to put in work on 3 key governors that has been a thorn in the side of the crazy President.

In this chapter the power crazy President Thumpf captures the Vice Pres , 1st Lady and their 2 friends. All the while during the melee the Pantha packs are injured trying to keep their moms out of harms way. Frequency has now joined the group and he brings them to the aftermath with healing and a decisive plan of bloody revenge.

This is the story of how the animals are severely injured. And Frequency uses the knowledge of DocBot to fix their injuries and connect the animals to their owners

Frequency Hunter is transformed back to his human form and joins the Pantha Pack to get revenge on everyone.